SPIRITUAL STORMS

Conquest over Crisis

Cedric Oliver

REAP
Publications

SPIRITUAL STORMS

Conquest over Crisis

Cedric Oliver

SPIRITUAL STORMS

CEDRIC OLIVER

REAP Publications
Indiana

SPIRITUAL STORMS

Conquest over Crisis

© Copyright 2005

Library of Congress Cataloging-in-Publication Data

Cedric Oliver

Spiritual Storms

ISBN: 0-9769912-0-9
1. Christians – Religious Life.
Printed in the United States of America

Anthony KaDarrell Thigpen,
Copy, Design, and Layout Editor
Clara Blackmon, Assistant Copy Editor
Cover Design by Swayzene Douglas

Printing by Jones Publishing Network—1.866.895.2268

DEDICATION

To all Christians who have withstood stormy times,
continue to be an example, forging a clear path for
others to follow. This is my tribute to you!

-ACKNOWLEDGMENTS-

I worship and thank God; our Father, the Lord Jesus Christ, and the Holy Spirit for His unceasing patience and love toward me. I'm also thankful because He has given my life meaning and purpose by including me in His eternal plan to bring heaven on earth.

Dear Joyce, my beautiful and wonderful wife of twenty-nine years – thank you. I can not adequately express how much I treasure your love for me. You continuously encourage me to pursue my destiny. You are my best friend – enduring life's most difficult challenges and celebrating every victory. I'm confident that every reader blessed by this book will experience the work God is accomplishing through our union.

To my precious daughter, Joy, thank you for believing in your daddy. Your love and support of my life in ministry is one of the strongest anchors that steady me during turbulent times. Your well-timed office "drop-bys" encourage me more than you'll ever know. You've become a beautiful woman before my eyes. I love you in a way only true fathers will ever understand.

To mom and dad, thanks for providing the environment that fostered the fulfillment of God's plan for my life. I honestly can't imagine where I would be today without your love, support, and guidance. I deeply love and appreciate you both.

A special thanks to my brothers Mike and Lawrence II, along with your loving wives and children. I honor your faithfulness and diligence. Thank you for standing with us in the ministry. I'm so grateful that we serve God and His people together. After all these years, we're closer than ever.

Embassies of Christ Kingdom Ministries, this book is born out of the words God graciously whispered to you. Thank you for praying, standing, and supporting Pastor Joyce and myself amid spiritual storms. Each of you played a significant part in making this book a reality. Trying to name each of you would be a bit intimidating. As we continue fulfilling God's vision through ministry, love one another as Christ loves us. I am deeply honored to pastor such a wonderful church. I love you all.

To my editor, Anthony KaDarrell Thigpen, thank you for stirring up the gift in me. Because of your help developing my thoughts and assistance writing this book, my dream has become a reality. Your passion, energy, and enthusiasm for this project inspired me to complete it.

CONTENTS

SPIRITUAL STORMS

Conquest over Crisis

- INTRODUCTION -

There is much for us to learn. Wouldn't life be like a cool summer breeze if we could go through each day trouble-free? Let's not allow our imaginations to drift too far. Reality assures us that we will suffer difficulties. Spiritual storms are troublesome times that all people inevitably face.

As an inner-city church pastor, I've rejoiced watching many sinners walk the aisles approaching the altar in tears to repent. Unfortunately, many people struggling with various issues share similar persuasions. They often think, "After I give my life to Jesus, my troubles will be over." Nothing could be farther from the truth.

There are indeed substantial supernatural benefits having a relationship with Christ. But challenges will frequently occur. Ultimately, upon repentance, God forgives our sins and gives us the promise of eternal life with Him. Hallelujah! In addition, through the gift of the Holy Spirit, we experience the nature, power, and authority of God, even during this present life on earth. This is God's plan of salvation.

Through Jesus Christ we have been granted dominion to rule and subdue the earth. As believers, we are "more than conquerors." We have been empowered to heal the sick, cast out devils, and raise the dead. We also have this assurance, *"God will supply every need of ours according to his riches in glory"* **Philippians 4:19**.

Despite this multitude of benefits, on occasion, things are prone to go wrong. "Why?" That's one question we've all asked? And that's one of many questions this book will answer. Why can't we simply speak to our crisis during storms and say, "Peace, be still!" Jesus did it, right? Why did God give us power, and simultaneously allow life's storms to wreak havoc. Why must we endure difficult times?

Certainly we've all experienced storms that frequently produce unwanted and unexpected occurrences in our lives. This book will explain why they come, how to escape them, and what happens when they leave.

Jesus makes it crystal clear, *"I have told you these things, so that in me you may have peace. In this* world you will have trouble. But take heart. I have overcome the world" **John 16:33**.

The Bible defines trouble as complicated times, or enduring persecution. Jesus explains to His followers that trouble is inevitable - even for "do gooders," if there are such people. Storms are in route, so it's important to prepare and position ourselves to come out victoriously.

If we don't understand and practice God's word, the outcome of storms can be devastating. The Bible says, "My people are destroyed for their lack of knowledge" **Hosea 4:6**. Different types of storms produce similar results, but they come into our lives for various reasons. One important Bible lesson we're soon to explore is that all storms are not alike.

The Bible teaches us that even Jesus Christ endured storms. "That day when evening came, he said to his disciples, "Let us go over to the other side" **Mark 4:35-41**. Leaving the crowd behind, they sailed onward. A furious gust of wind caused strong waves to break over the boat. Jesus was in the stern sleeping on a cushion. The disciples woke him and said, "Teacher, don't you care if we drown?" He got up, rebuked the wind, and said to the waves, "Quiet! (peace) Be still!" Then the violent wind stopped blowing and the atmosphere became completely calm. Jesus said to his disciples, "Why are you so afraid? Do you still have no faith?" They were terrified and asked each other, "Who is this? Even the wind and the waves obey him!" Since everything Jesus says comes to pass, we might imagine that their boat ride would have been hassle-free. "Does Jesus lead us into difficult situations," some might ask? Sometimes He does and at other times we cause chaos ourselves.

Storms will prevent us from walking in our destiny if we're not focused. As they sailed through the night, dangerous winds started blowing. Jesus and His disciples encountered an unexpected storm of great force that attempted to prevent them from arriving to their destination. The force of the storm appeared to be physical in nature, but its source was spiritual. An unleashed satanic scheme attempted to prevent Jesus from accomplishing what He purposed in His heart to do. Ultimately, Jesus' destiny destroyed the works of the devil.

It's not in Satan's nature to stand by and give

Jesus a free pass to bring glory to God? That's unequivocally not the way the enemy operates. The devil is an opposing force determined to do anything to prevent God's kingdom from advancing. Although Christ proves himself to be more than a conqueror, Satan's most potent weapon attempted to stop Jesus – a great storm.

The boat began tossing and turning. Strong waves started causing rushing water to quickly flow into the rapidly flooding vessel. Seemingly shipwrecked, the drifting boat appeared to be sinking. Jesus' disciples panicked and chaos climaxed. They'd previously seen Jesus perform miracles, but their confidence failed when their faith was tested.

The disciples also seemed to forget the power Christ displayed when he healed the man with leprosy. No one even mentioned the episode of Jesus restoring the man suffering with a withered hand. These memories seem to have cringed and crawled deep into the corners of their minds. That's what happens to our faith when we're not prepared for spiritual storms. The disciples were totally disoriented, both physically and spiritually. Confusion caused them to lose sight of Jesus' purpose and power. They seemed to have forgotten that Jesus, asleep on deck, possessed divine authority. Then again, perhaps they didn't think Jesus possessed power over this particular situation. We've all questioned God's willingness to change our circumstances at some point in our lives.

For a brief moment, it appeared that this storm accomplished its objective. But Jesus' response proved otherwise. Instead of running, panicking, and trying to bale-out water, He slept. Wasn't Jesus in the same storm as the disciples? Surely he must have been soaking wet from the splashing waves, yet He was not concerned. What did Jesus know about the storm that the disciples were not aware of? Why was He able to keep His composure and respond verbally as opposed to reacting physically?

Jesus possessed an insightful revelation about life's storms. He understands the spiritual source of storms and controls there physical outcomes. Jesus does not fight with flesh. Instead, He responds with spiritual maturity.

Jesus also knew the purpose of His personal storms He faced – faith must be tested. Jesus prevailed during the time of testing, and so can we. He didn't allow storm-like circumstances to prevent him from fulfilling God's purpose. Instead, He took control of the situation and continued sailing toward His destination. He thought quickly and operated in His spiritual authority. The life-threatening storm did not intimidate Christ.

We're able to learn countless lessons from this passage of scripture. If Jesus, the King of kings, and Lord of lords, faced storms, what causes us to expect that we won't face storms during our lives? It's not a matter of "if"; it's a matter of "when" storms will occur.

It is my prayer that this book will equip and empower people of faith to successfully go through, and if necessary, get out of unwarranted storms. The principles we'll explore throughout in this book will enable readers to find the shortest path to peace and victory. Jesus made it to the other side; beyond the storm to His destination, and so can we.

We will also discover the source, purpose, dura-tion, and most importantly, a way of escape from various storm categories. A category 1 storm whirls out of disobedience, rebellion, and sin. A category 2 storm spirals from faithfulness and spiritual maturity. A category 3 storm is internal turmoil, and a category 4 storm starts because of pride and idolatrous living.

That's how we'll identify each storm for the purpose of gaining a shared perspective. Each storm should be approached with a Christ-like attitude, but every storm produces a different outcome. Successfully navigating through storms require properly identifying the category type. We must honestly evaluate ourselves to determine where we are in our spiritual growth. Afterward, our success depends on how well we follow instructions.

I've personally experienced each storm category. I'm not proud of my past mistakes, rebellion, or pride. However, if sharing various episodes of my private life helps others, then to God, be all glory.

I'm familiar with the bitter feelings, arrogant thought processes, and attitudes that cause each storm to blow into our lives. Within this book, I've disclosed former weaknesses that delayed my progress of getting to my current destination. I've also shared personal testimonies God used to redeem time and help me fulfill my destiny.

As we discover more about the nature of spiritual storms, we will be able to navigate through them with a clear exit strategy. No longer need Christians feel disoriented, confused, and hopeless. Be assured, no matter what type of storm we face, God has already provided a way of escape!

CHAPTER 1

- NOBODY'S EXEMPT -
Life's twists and turns

- NOBODY'S EXEMPT -

In the midst of personal dilemmas, world chaos, poverty, and confusion, most people wonder, "Where is God?" Non-believers have even questioned, "If there is a God, why does He allow bad things to happen to helpless people?" While gazing in shock at CNN's August 2004 news reports about Hurricane Charley, many viewers watched the devastating storm slam into Florida. Only months later, December 26, a powerful undersea earthquake in the Indian Ocean triggered a devastating tsunami that killed more than 212,000 people, according to CNN World News Reports. April 26, 2005, while recovering from the initial flood, the same geographical region experienced a similar tragedy. Imagine.

Try to empathize with victims returning to their neighborhoods only to gaze at death's disaster. What would be our reaction if our houses were completely leveled to the ground, family members missing, and the stench of dead bodies filtered the air? Also, imagine having to triumph over the threat of deadly diseases, homelessness, starvation, and broken families. Some people even suffered additional agonies that the media neglected to premiere. How would we cope with the internal pain caused by the external disaster? This questions seems almost impossible to answer. Our ministry felt compelled to pray. Afterward, we immediately sent financial support to help aid in various relief efforts. Unfortunately, money can't replace the tragic loss of entire families and villages.

Such a catastrophe would probably cause most people to experience emotional and psychological devastation. It's tragic to be a victim of a physical storm. Although, it requires another kind of strength to handle the spiraling force of spiritual chaos. Spiritual storms are just as devastating as natural storms, and even worse, if we don't know how to handle them. God has empowered me to resurrect this revelation on stormy times – Spiritual Storms.

There are different types of spiritual storms. Most believers think they're experiencing an unwarranted attack from the devil, but that's not always the case. This book will help readers regain focus in the midst of challenges and prepare for future difficulties. It will also help Christians avoid unwanted and meaningless struggles.

Different storms have different purposes. That's why we have to understand the source of our storms. "Why is this happening to me?" This seems to be a prayer God seldom answers. He doesn't divulge answers while the quiz is in progress. Storms only happen after God has given us the tools needed to succeed.

There are many things we're soon to discover about storms in the lives of believers. We'll also consider questions like, "What authority do I have when I'm going through a storm" and "How long will this mess last?" Some believers feel they have total authority over all storms, but life experiences prove that's not true. Our individual decisions often determine the duration of our spiritual storms.

FOUNDATIONAL SCRIPTURE

Mark 4:35-38 (NIV)
That day when evening came, he said to his disciples, "Let us go over to the other side." [36] Leaving the crowd behind, they took him along, just as he was, in the boat. There were also other boats with him. [37] A furious squall came up, and the waves broke over the boat, so that it was nearly

swamped. [38] Jesus was in the stern, sleeping on a cushion. The disciples woke him and said to him, "Teacher, don't you care if we drown?"

The first lesson this scripture teaches us is that Jesus Himself was not exempt from storms. Even Jesus Christ experienced twists and turns. The gospel of Mark highlights a physical storm, but the account represents difficult times, nonetheless.

According to the gospels, religious groups tried to kill Jesus at birth. And their efforts continued throughout His ministry. His enemies even sent chaotic crowds and squads of soldiers to incite riots against Him. They accused Jesus of conducting public teachings that conflicted with their traditional understanding of the law. Once again, Jesus was not exempt from stormy times and neither are we.

We are destined to experience storms. Jesus assures us that our lifetime will not be trouble free. Storms will occur. The effect of a natural storm is when the normal turbulence is interrupted. Spiritual storms create similar devastating consequences - our normal flow of life becomes drastically disturbed. Isn't it interesting that the theory behind natural storms supports spiritual storms? Research shows, most people learn more often from the visuals that surround us. So, let's take a closer look at our lives and examine ourselves.

When the storm arose while the disciples were on the boat, there were two different responses. Jesus' disciples reacted one way and He responded another. In fact, when the storm arose, the disciples lost hope, even though Jesus was present. So, if strong winds whip hard enough, or the boat rocks rough enough, it's possible for even the elect in Christ to lose ground.

Oftentimes, followers of Christ fail to exercise faith. As a result, we think certain situations aren't going to work out successfully. How can we not make it through difficult times victoriously, if Christ, who cannot fail, is in the same boat with us? We must learn to trust Him.

Again, spiritual storms have different sources. Believers tend to think that the devil initiates all storms, but that's only partially accurate. The devil does not initiate all of our storms, sometimes we start them. It's an unpopular theory, but we're often the cause of our own problems. This book will help readers better prepare for the inevitable and avoid the unnecessary.

We're either going through a storm, we've just triumphed over one, or its fierce winds are blowing in our direction. Now, let's target the characteristics of the four categories of storms mentioned.

CHAPTER 2

Category 1 Storm:

- THE FUGITIVE -
Jonah's disobedience and rebellion

- THE FUGITIVE -

Old Testament prophet Jonah, known best by his grueling experience in the belly of a whale, serves as a great example of disobedience and rebellion.

Don't deliberate in judgment of Jonah. Surely, Jonah and I aren't the only ones who have rebelled against God's instruction.

Jonah 1:1-3 (NIV)
The word of the Lord came to Jonah son of Amittai: [2] "Go to the great city of Nineveh and preach against it, because its wickedness has come up before me." [3] But Jonah ran away from the Lord and headed for Tarshish. He went down to Joppa, where he found a ship bound for that port. After paying the fare, he went aboard and sailed for Tarshish to flee from the Lord.

Jonah's experience defines one of many descriptive examples of a category 1 storm. He ran away from the Lord. Running from God, His people, and the church, is an early indicator of a category 1 storm.

Surely we've all asked, "Why is all of this chaos

going on in my life?" Well, when we experience a category 1 storm; running away from God's good discretion, there's nobody to blame but ourselves. We go through this type of severe trouble because of something we've done wrong. A category 1 storm will start spinning into our lives when we are disobedient, rebellious, or outright sinful. It's caused by poor decisions, not the devil's doing.

This reminds me of how we make bad choices thinking our decisions are based on valid reasons. My wife and I, have served in ministry all of our lives. We understand many Bible principles based on firsthand experiences, particularly in areas of tithes and offering. We learned the importance of giving faithfully when we were teenagers. Although we individually reaped countless blessings directly based on our giving, difficult times challenged our faith as newlyweds. Years ago, financial instabilities resulting from inconsistent tithing, taught us a well-deserved lesson.

At age twenty, Joyce said "I do" and agreed to dedicate the rest of her life to me in holy matrimony! Her beauty was just as irresistible back then as it is today. But good looks and charming personalities don't detour unwanted storms. The year 1976 marked the beginning of difficult times for us.

> **The exit strategy out of a category 1 storm is to realign your life with the word of God.**

We didn't have the privilege of pre-marital counseling. Perhaps if we did, our first few years of marriage would not have posed such frustrating financial hardships. It seemed like we would take one step forward and three steps backward, financially. Something unexpected always happened and we'd find our bank account short of needed funds. We were frustrated because past due monthly payments kept rapidly accumulating.

We prayed together. We confessed prosperity over our finances. We put **Malachi 3:10** to memory, *Bring the whole tithe into the storehouse, that there may be food in my house. Test me in this, says the Lord Almighty, and see if I will not throw open the floodgates of heaven and pour out so much blessing that you will not have room enough for it.*

We kept giving and believing, but we didn't receive expected results as quickly as we'd hoped to. As time progressed, our situation got worse and we made a poor decision. Like Jonah, we disobeyed God and took matters into our own hands. We devised a plan of our own.

We decided to stop giving tithes for just one month. Seems simple enough, right? We logically decided to use our tithes to catch up on some late bills. Although we knew better, for that brief moment we failed to realize that God's instructions produce better results than our plans. We were so nervous. It was clear to us that we were walking in disobedience. Our decision directly conflicted with God's word. Yet, we forged ahead anyway, following the sinful shortcut we devised to gain some economic relief.

Within days, our hot water heater malfunctioned. Coincident, I think not! The cost of the replacement equaled the amount of our tithes we neglected to give. Our finances quickly spiraled out of control. And wouldn't you know it, instead of things getting better, we found ourselves in a category 1 storm.

We knew this storm was raging because of our

direct disobedience to God's word. So, we didn't even see the need to wonder why our circumstances started twisting and turning even worse. We repented quickly, pleading God's forgiveness. I remember waiting anxiously for our next pay checks so that we could redeem our giving. Our finances immediately began to improve. Since then, we've always given God what belongs to Him. In fact, now we cheerfully give much higher than ten

> **Category 1 storms happen when we make decisions that conflict with the word of God.**

percent. It wasn't until we passed the test that God elevated our finances to another level.

For years, we've been financially stable because God blesses our faithfulness. Now our giving exceeds the total amount of our previous annual income. But back then, we couldn't see our future clearly, so, we staggered in disobedience and rebellion. When we decided to obey God, the storm stopped and our finances increased. We learned from this personal experience that the exit strategy out of a category 1 storm is to realign your life with the word of God.

Let's revisit the city of Nineveh and take a closer look at the life of Jonah. Notice that the devil didn't send this particular storm. Jonah disappointed God when he disobeyed and rebelled.

Afterward, God created a gust of wind and blew it in Jonah's direction. The storm arose because of Jonah's decision to rebel. Modern day Christians tend to overlook this profound truth. When we've started our own storm, we can scream until we're blue in the face, "Peace! Be still!" But this storm will not calm until we repent. Until then, we should expect this type of storm to continue.

Some believers say they don't accept Old Testament teachings, but the principle of sowing and reaping is still active. Farmers continue to experience seed time and harvest, because of this principle. Even in this dispensation of grace, if we continue to live in disobedience and rebellion, we'll reap the consequences. Whatever a man sows he shall also reap. This New Testament scripture helps us discover why certain things take place in our

> **A Category 1 storm comes when we do the opposite of what God instructs us to.**

lives. Even though Jonah was an Old Testament prophet of God, he reaped the penalty of disobedience. This is how the principle of sowing and reaping works and there is no way around it.

Judges 3:7-8, 12-14 (NIV)
The Israelites did evil in the eyes of the Lord; they forgot the Lord their God and served the Baals and the Asherahs. [8] The anger of the Lord burned against Israel so that he sold them into the hands of Cushan-Rishathaim king of Aram Naharaim, to whom the Israelites were subject for eight years. [12] Once again the Israelites did evil in the eyes of the Lord, and because they did this evil the Lord gave Eglon king of Moab power over Israel. [13] Getting the Ammonites and Amalekites to join him, Eglon came and attacked Israel, and they took possession of the City of Palms. [14] The Israelites were subject to Eglon king of Moab for eighteen years.

The source of a category 1 storm is the permissive will of God. It happens when we make decisions that conflict with His word. When the chosen people of God did evil in the sight of the Lord, God allowed them to be overtaken by their enemies. As with the Israelites, God does not wink His

> **Disobedience and rebellion will invite a category 1 storm.**

eye of approval at our mis-
chievous acts.

> **God wants us to totally rely on Him, instead of our independent resources.**

If we defy God, evil will
come into our lives. It's
our individual decision to
obey or disobey – this is
the nature of freewill. God
allows us to make choices, and our decisions
dictate our future. God will not twist our arms and
pry His knee into our spines, forcing us to obey.

God is not evil; however, he allows evil to test our
faith during a category 1 storm. When we hide
ourselves in His perfect will, we're protected. God
desires to teach us in love, not destroy us in anger.
After the children of Israel were freed from eight
years of bondage, they made the same mistake
again. As a result, God allowed them to go into
bondage an additional eighteen years. We must
ask ourselves how often do we make the same
mistake twice? Our answer to this question will
help us understand why certain areas of our lives
are stifled.

A category 1 storm comes when we do the opposite of what God instructs us to. Disobedience causes Satan to gain authority over us. The Bible says we become servants of whoever we obey. The judgment was even more severe the second time the

> **In a category 1 storm, we're only one decision away from causing the storm to stop.**

Israelites rebelled against God. So, it would not have made any sense for them to ask, "What are we doing here," or "Why is all of this chaos going on in our lives?" We are where we are in life because of the choices we've made. But it's never too late to change. Again, we shouldn't waste time and energy blaming the devil for a category 1 storm. There's only one person that can cause this type of storm to come into our lives - we create it ourselves. We should search our hearts and examine our lives to make sure we aren't starting storms.

Disobedience and rebellion will invite a category 1 storm. It happens because we're in the flesh, and our human impulses desire to feed carnal urges. It wars against the will of God. Natural desires reject and resist God's word.

Whatever God makes is good. In fact, He designed our natural senses so great, that during this human experience we gravitate toward earthly desires. So, as long as we're in this fleshly body we're going to have to fight! We must keep our guards up and remain ready to rumble! We have to kill the urges that defy the word of God. The Apostle Paul said, "I die daily." Either we're going to obey God or we're going to obey carnal urges. That decision is left up to us. If we obey our urges, then we disobey God, and a storm is coming – there's no way to avoid this principle.

2 Samuel 24:1, 10-13 (NIV)
Again the anger of the Lord burned against Israel, and he incited David against them, saying, "Go and take a census of Israel and Judah." [10] David was conscience-stricken after he had counted the fighting men, and he said to the Lord, "I have sinned greatly in what I have done. Now, O Lord, I beg you, take away the guilt of your servant. I have done a very foolish thing." [11] Before David got up the next morning, the word of the Lord had come to Gad the prophet, David's seer: [12] "Go and tell David, 'This is what the Lord says: I am giving you three options. Choose one of them for me to carry out against you.'" [13] So Gad went to David and said to him, "Shall there come upon you three years of famine in your land? Or three months of fleeing from your enemies while they

pursue you? Or three days of plague in your land? Now then, think it over and decide how I should answer the one who sent me."

God wanted David to solely depend on Him instead of an army of men. Likewise, God wants us to totally rely on Him, instead of our independent resources. Even after David admitted his sin, God penalized him with natural consequences. When David repented, God gave him a choice between three severe penalties. Although he had choices, David didn't escape having to endure consequences. Neither will we be able to avoid the penalty for our acts of disobedience. God is merciful and patient. And surely, we've all made sinful mistakes, but a rebellious lifestyle will incite a storm.

We sometimes wonder why our finances, family, and friends seem to create chaos in our lives. Maybe we should routinely evaluate ourselves and ask, "In what area of my life have I chosen to disobey God?"

We can verbally rebuke the devil on a daily basis, but the reason this storm occurs is because God permits it, not Satan. This is why an acclamation of faith appears ineffective, such as "Peace! Be Still!" It's beneficial for us to learn how to accept what God allows. Storms reveal God's judgment when we fail. When we are in a category 1 storm, we have no spiritual authority over our situation. As long as disobedience reigns in us, we can't stop this storm. Even the most anointed and powerful evangelical prayer line can't stop a category 1 storm.

We must make a decision to repent and change before God gives us authority to dictate prosperous outcomes. When we're in a category 1 storm, we're only one decision away from causing the storm to stop. Remember, this storm will last until we repent. And by the way, crying is not repentance. Repentance is changing our outlook and making a decision to obey God. Everyone has needed a second chance at some point in life. Repentance lends us an opportunity to turn this storm into success.

CHAPTER 3

Category 2 Storm:

- THIS IS ONLY A TEST -
Job's righteousness and maturity

- THIS IS ONLY A TEST -

Acategory 2 storm is quite different from others. This storm is based on the fact that God is about to bless us for our spiritual maturity. God rewards the diligence of those who seek and obey Him, **Hebrews 11:6.**

As we've learned from chapter 2, there are absolutely no benefits of going through a category 1 storm. Afterward, God redirects us to go back and fulfill His initial command. We have to start at our last act of disobedience. During a category 1 storm we lose ground unnecessarily.

On the other hand, a category 2 storm is almost impossible to anticipate – it suddenly happens in God's timing.

Genesis 37:3-28 (NIV)
Now Israel loved Joseph more than any of his other sons, because he had been born to him in his old age; and he made a richly ornamented robe for him. [4] When his brothers saw that

Storms have a way of causing us to examine ourselves, even when we're doing the right thing.

> **God rewards the diligence of those who seek and obey Him.**

their father loved him more than any of them, they hated him and could not speak a kind word to him. [5] Joseph had a dream, and when he told it to his brothers, they hated him all the more. [6] He said to them, "Listen to this dream I had: [7] We were binding sheaves of grain out in the field when suddenly my sheaf rose and stood upright, while your sheaves gathered around mine and bowed down to it." [8] His brothers said to him, "Do you intend to reign over us? Will you actually rule us?" And they hated him all the more because of his dream and what he had said. [9] Then he had another dream, and he told it to his brothers. "Listen," he said, "I had another dream, and this time the sun and moon and eleven stars were bowing down to me." [10] When he told his father as well as his brothers, his father rebuked him and said, "What is this dream you had? Will your mother and I and your brothers actually come and bow down to the ground before you?" [11] His brothers were jealous of him, but his father kept the matter in mind. [12] Now his brothers had gone to graze their father's flocks near Shechem, [13] and Israel said to Joseph, "As you know, your brothers are grazing the flocks near Shechem. Come, I am going to send you to them.""Very well," he replied. [14] So he said to him, "Go and see if all is well with your brothers and with the flocks, and bring word back to me." Then he sent him off from the Valley of Hebron. When Joseph arrived at Shechem, [15] a man found him wandering around in the fields and asked him, "What are you looking for?" [16] He replied, "I'm looking for my brothers. Can you tell me where they are grazing their flocks?" [17] "They have moved on from here," the man answered. "I heard them say, 'Let's go to Dothan.' "So Joseph went after his brothers and found them near Dothan. [18] But they saw him in the distance, and before he reached them, they plotted to kill him. [19] "Here comes that dreamer!" they said to each other. [20] "Come now, let's kill him and throw him into one of these cisterns and say that a ferocious animal devoured him. Then we'll see what comes of his dreams." [21] When Reuben heard this, he tried to rescue him from their hands. "Let's not take his life," he said. [22] "Don't shed any blood. Throw him into this cistern here in the desert, but don't lay a hand on him." Reuben said this to rescue him from them and take him back to his father. [23] So when Joseph came to his brothers, they stripped him of his robe--the richly ornamented robe he was wearing- [24] and they took him and threw him into the cistern. Now the cistern was empty; there was no water in it. [25] As they sat down to eat their meal, they looked up and saw a caravan of Ishmaelites coming from Gilead.

God has a purpose for every storm.

Their camels were loaded with spices, balm and myrrh, and they were on their way to take them down to Egypt. [26] Judah said to his brothers, "What will we gain if we kill our brother and cover up his blood? [27] Come, let's sell him to the Ishmaelites and not lay our hands on him; after all, he is our brother, our own flesh and blood." His brothers agreed. [28] So when the Midianite merchants came by, his brothers pulled Joseph up out of the cistern and sold him for twenty shekels of silver to the Ishmaelites, who took him to Egypt.

> **Faithful Christians are not exempt from the tragedies of severe storms.**

Joseph's biological brothers were jealous of him. They threw him in a deep pit, and then sold him into slavery. He experienced a vile storm. Joseph was a righteous man, according to scripture. He obeyed God and made upright decisions, but his brothers despised him. Have you ever encountered the force of a storm even after obeying God's specific instructions? Storms have a way of causing us to examine ourselves, even when we think we're doing the right thing.

When we know we've done something wrong, the guilt of our rebellious actions is difficult to hide.

During these episodes in life, we expect a storm. But a category 2 storm is often unexpected. It hits like a tornado. Meteorologists are equipped to give far more advance warnings for hurricanes than torna-

> **God always has something greater in store than what meets our eyes.**

does. Such is the case with spiritual storms, some we expect, and others we don't. Unfortunately, the majority of storms Christians face don't occur from spiritual maturity. Generally, believers are able to pinpoint where they veered off track. But not Joseph and Job, they were perfect and upright men.

Job 1:1, 6-12, 22 (NIV)
In the land of Uz there lived a man whose name was Job. This man was blameless and upright; he feared God and shunned evil. [6] One day the angels came to present themselves before the Lord, and Satan also came with them. [7] The Lord said to Satan, "Where have you come from?" Satan answered the Lord, "From roaming through the earth and going back and forth in it." [8] Then the Lord said to Satan, "Have you considered my servant Job? There is no one on earth like him; he is blameless and upright, a man who fears God and shuns evil." [9] "Does Job fear God for noth-

ing?" Satan replied. [10] "Have you not put a hedge around him and his household and everything he has? You have blessed the work of his hands, so that his flocks and herds are spread throughout the land. [11] But stretch out your hand and strike everything he has, and he will surely curse you to your face." [12] The Lord said to Satan, "Very well, then, everything he has is in your hands, but on the man himself do not lay a finger." Then Satan went out from the presence of the Lord. [22] In all this, Job did not sin by charging God with wrongdoing.

This type of storm does not seem to make common sense – it doesn't appear to be based on sound logic. It seems as though when we're doing everything right, we shouldn't be exposed to a storm, but God has a purpose for it. Job was a blameless man, according to the Bible, but he lost everything – from family and cattle to land. Before Job could get to the end of one situation, the next wave of the storm tumbled into his life. This also makes it clear that faithful Christians are not exempt from the tragedies of severe storms. We have to prepare for the unexpected. Old Testament prophet Daniel is another example of an individual who faced unanticipated challenges with courage. Like Joseph and Job, he also encountered a category 2 storm.

Daniel 6:1-7 (NIV)

It pleased Darius to appoint 120 satraps to rule throughout the kingdom, [2] with three administrators over them, one of whom was Daniel. The satraps were made accountable to them so that the king might not suffer loss. [3] Now Daniel so distinguished himself among the administrators and the satraps by his exceptional qualities that the king planned to set him over the whole kingdom. [4] At this, the administrators and the satraps tried to find grounds for charges against Daniel in his conduct of government affairs, but they were unable to do so. They could find no corruption in him, because he was trustworthy and neither corrupt nor negligent. [5] Finally these men said, "We will never find any basis for charges against this man Daniel unless it has something to do with the law of his God." [6] So the administrators and the satraps went as a group to the king and said: "O King Darius, live forever! [7] The royal administrators, prefects, satraps, advisers and governors have all agreed that the king should issue an edict and enforce the decree that anyone who prays to any god or man during the next thirty days, except to you, O king, shall be thrown into the lions' den.

Daniel's enemies scrutinized him and they were still unable to find fault. He was trustworthy. He was not corrupt. And neither was he negligent in responsibility. So, jealous rulers of less stature devised a plan that landed Daniel in a cave of lions. Daniel made a decision not to disobey God's law. Because of the rebellious nature of our flesh, it's important that we remain determined to stand on God's word. Nonetheless, the jealousy of others landed Daniel in a pit. This is merely one of many examples of how a category 2 storm starts. Daniel's reward for being upright seemed to be a lions' den experience. But God always has something greater in store than what meets our eyes.

Luke 3:21 (NIV)
When all the people were being baptized, Jesus was baptized too. And as he was praying, heaven was opened.

Luke 4:1-2 (NIV)
Jesus, full of the Holy Spirit, returned from the Jordan and was led by the Spirit in the desert, [2] where for forty days he was tempted by the devil. He ate nothing during those days, and at the end of them he was hungry.

Although God was well pleased with Jesus, He sent him on a wilderness experience. This type of storm confuses Christians. I've heard so many financial givers say to me, "It seems like when I started tithing, my financial situation got worse." Others have said, "Pastor, every since I started confessing healing over my sickness it seems like the pain is getting worse." Ultimately, these types of responses echo from the same experience. In other words they were asking, "Why am I not getting the expected results when I do the right thing?"

I'm familiar with that question. Upon earning my MBA after graduate school, I was promoted to operations manager of one of the largest departments in my company. Even as a Spirit-filled believer, the new position was overwhelming. I was the company's first African-American ever to control a $53 million operating budget, along with a $42 million upgrade project. With no doubt, all eyes were on me. In fact, squinted eyes, clinched fists, and crossed fingers best describes the disposition of jealous naysayers. On the other hand, there were others hoping I'd succeed.

I remained prayerful. This new journey ushered me into the presence of God unlike never before. I realized that my success relied solely on God's guidance. I avoided carnality, and walked closely with the Lord. I examined myself thoroughly to insure that my life was in line with God's word.

The Holy Spirit assured me, "I would never put you

anywhere to fail." As a result, I began tackling oppositions that accompanied my new position. Faith destined me for success. After about a year of planning, we launched the implementation phase of our $42 million facility upgrade.

We encountered more obstacles than anticipated. Needed installation experts had been reassigned to other high-budget projects due to our one year delay.

The second string of installation experts weren't nearly as versed on the equipment as their predecessors. I stayed prayerful, believing that all things were going to work out for my good. When the engineers arrived, the installation appeared to be going extremely well. We were maintaining the new timelines and precisely allocating the funds in our budget. My superiors were exceedingly pleased with my leadership on the project.

Examine yourself thoroughly to insure that your life is in line with God's word.

After workers completed the equipment installation, a sequence of operational tests began. To my surprise, we discovered serious problems. Nothing worked properly. The installation failed. My engineers reviewed the blueprints to insure each step was completed according to guidelines. The team of engineers couldn't locate any reason for the apparent malfunctions. As a result, the equipment manufacturers rushed to our rescue, but their efforts proved helpless, also. Everything was done right, but everything was going wrong.

For the next year, my department lost between $1-2 million per month. My superiors were demanding solutions. Work became my greatest stress. I felt more pressure daily. Circumstances forced me to contact our chief executive officer weekly, and conduct bi-weekly action plans with our chief operation officer. We scratched the surface of many alternate plans, but the new equipment remained counter-productive. I followed proper procedures, but nothing worked no matter how many experts helped.

I empathized with King David the psalmist; it seemed my enemies were waiting to watch me fall. And the situation assured them that I was soon to fail. I often paced the department floor praying in the spirit. My hair started turning gray. My faith, I thought had been stretched to its limit. While others calculated our financial losses, I took inventory of my life, once again. I pondered, "Is there any area of disobedience in my life that opened the door for Satan to bring this storm?" I couldn't think of anything. Then I questioned God, "Why is this happening to me?"

Over 365-days of torment drifted swiftly like a desert sand storm – tedious and troublesome. Still, we gained no territory in our endless attempts of locating an effective solution. At the time, this was the most severe storm I ever encountered.

I imagined that my superiors were rethinking my position. But I kept holding God accountable in my prayers. I said, "You promised that you would never put me anywhere to fail." I never accepted defeat, and continued to confess success. Rumors spread when various employees started gossiping about my expected demotion. After losing nearly $15 million and having every technical resource give up on the project, again, I prayed.

Late one night God spoke. His words seemed simple, but specific. He gave me instructions detailing what changes to make in the department. God said, "Go back to the old way." Instantly, I knew exactly what He meant! His words seemed elementary - extremely easy to understand. I immediately responded, "Yes, Lord, I'll do it first thing in the morning."

The next morning, upon arriving to work, I called an unexpected staff meeting. I disseminated the instructions to "go back to the old way" of doing things. And O' boy, did muffled voices growl in disagreement. Blank stares served as companions to the fowl attitudes of those in disbelief. The criticism flared almost unbearably. Everyone told me it couldn't be done. They explained that the new equipment was not designed to operate using old procedures. It was unheard of. Some workers even said I was going to make matters even worse. I gave the final word, "The plan is not up for discussion, implement it immediately. Go back to the old way!" The meeting concluded, God's plan was put into action, and to everyone's surprise it worked!

From that day forward, we gradually gained daily progress. Our department broke historical produc-tion records and became one of the most profit-

able in the company. Our losses seemed to have
been forgotten and written off as a thing of the
past. Company executives mapped out my future
career anticipating that I'd quickly climb to the top.
I knew God was responsible, even though executives accredited me for the overwhelming success.
I gave praise to God.

So, what was the purpose of this storm? It proved
to be for testing and promotion, both naturally and
spiritually. For five years, I'd been instructing my
congregation to walk by faith and not by sight. I
constantly repeated "No weapon formed against us
will prosper." I also reminded the church that the
word of God could not fail. I had been tested in
these areas before, but I had to pay the price for
teaching it to others. Jesus said trouble or persecution comes because of the word, **Matthew
13:21.** Every word we speak will be put to the
test!

God allows certain tests as a final preparation for promotion.

My storm wasn't nearly as
severe as Job's experience,
although the intensity
affected many areas of my
life. God allowed this particular test as my final
preparation for full-time

ministry.

Understanding God's foresight of our future should help us endure life's challenges with confidence. When we walk in obedience to God's plan, despite unwanted pressure, we're guaranteed to prosper. During this storm, I learned to listen and obey God's voice amid life's greatest challenges. I've also learned to follow Him regardless of what others have to say.

When we're going through a category 2 storm, it's caused by our level of spiritual maturity and faith. This storm doesn't happen unless we've had sufficient time to apply the word of God that we've been taught. At this point, some readers might think, "Well, I don't ever want to grow up spiritually!" While it would be nice if we could avoid growing pains, it's impossible.

Without growth, we'll experience dysfunction. And God desires that we live healthy lives, spiritually and naturally. So, He directs us in paths to fulfill our destiny. This is why we can't avoid storms. Whether we obey or rebel we'll encounter a suitable storm. Remember, we have an enemy. The devil presents himself before the Lord asking permission to destroy and test us. **Luke 22:31 (NIV)** *"Simon, Simon, Satan has asked to sift you as wheat."* Using Simon's scenario, Jesus reminds us that Satan's

There's no such thing as promotion without testing.

current desire is to sift us as wheat. Ultimately, the devil desires to kill, steal, and destroy us – he wants to annihilate God's people.

The purpose of a category 2 storm is testing and promotion. This storm comes into our lives because we have sufficient knowledge and faith to pass the test. There's no such thing as promotion without testing. Prior to students excelling to the next grade level they must pass certain academic requirements. We have to be prepared for "the next level." It's not just a Christian cliché?

Faith has to be tested. We can't continuously listen to anointed Bible teaching and intentionally not grow up spiritually. Our category 2 storm is on the way. In fact, stay prayerful, keep reading the bible, confess God's word, and don't forsake Church fellowship, because these tornado-like storms are inevitable.

Everyone wants to be a spiritual giant, but no one wants to be tested. The purpose of a test is not for God to know where our hearts are – it's for us to know. God already knows everything we're going to do. The bible says He's omniscient – God knows everything. Many churchgoers think they're spiritual giants, but as soon as a storm comes into their life, they're defeated by the unexpected. A lot of students go to school everyday, but fail to pay attention and get upset when teachers issue failing grades. Tests determine if we have to repeat a grade or move on to higher heights.

Never invite a storm. In other words, we should avoid thinking more highly of ourselves than we ought to. Zealous believers leap ahead of themselves prematurely and pretend they're somebody worth esteeming. We must remember that humility is one of our greatest assets as Christians. A spiritual storm will swiftly humble a high-minded and arrogant person.

> **The purpose of a test is not for God to know where our hearts are – it's for us to know.**

Matthew 13:21 (NIV)

But since he has no root, he lasts only a short time.

When trouble or persecution comes because of the word, he quickly falls away.

Trouble and persecution happens because of the word, according to scripture. After we hear the word of God, difficult times are sure to come. This storm will spring up specifically because we've been living right. Always remember that our right-eousness is of the Lord; Otherwise, we'll find ourselves standing on unstable ground.

1 Corinthians 10:12-13 (NIV)
So, if you think you are standing firm, be careful that you don't fall! [13] No temptation has seized you except what is common to man. And God is faithful; he will not let you be tempted beyond what you can bear. But when you are tempted, he will also provide a way out so that you can stand up under it.

When we're going through difficult times, we must always remember that God is faithful. God under-stands what we're going through. As with Job, God will allow the devil to touch our possessions, but Satan can't destroy our lives. This storm is only a test. We can make it through a category 2 storm, because God is faithful and he will not tempt or test us beyond what we can bear. He looks at our lives, hearts, and assesses our knowledge of His word against the severity of the storm. Stand strong, knowing that a just God is concerned about the outcome of our circumstances.

It's important to maintain the right attitude when we're going through a storm, especially this one.

Ephesians 6:13-18 (NIV)
Therefore put on the full armor of God, so that when the day of evil comes, you may be able to stand your ground, and after you have done everything, to stand. [14] Stand firm then, with the belt of truth buckled around your waist, with the breastplate of righteousness in place, [15] and with your feet fitted with the readiness that comes from the gospel of peace. [16] In addition to all this, take up the shield of faith, with which you can extinguish all the flaming arrows of the evil one. [17] Take the helmet of salvation and the sword of the Spirit, which is the word of God. [18] And pray in the Spirit on all occasions with all kinds of prayers and requests. With this in mind, be alert and always keep on praying for all the saints.

Regardless of what comes our way, we must continue living dedicated word-based lives. We must have our minds made up that we're going to stand on the word of God. This storm is not going anywhere until we successfully pass our test. As a

> **Regardless of what comes our way, we must continue living dedicated word-based lives.**

child, I would get angry when another student finished an exam about ten minutes into the test. I felt like growling, because it seemed such kids were show-offs. Now, I realize they were prepared for their promotion. We have to hide the word of God in our heart so that when the test comes we'll be ready. And if we effectively prepare, there will be no delays. Study the Bible and put the word into practice to gain expeditious victories.

Again, secondary education reminds us that if we fail too many tests, we forfeit promotion. This is the case with spiritual education as well. That's why church attendance serves an immeasurable importance. Otherwise, we'll miss out on critical information needed for spiritual tests – don't get held back.

Matthew 7:24-27 (NIV)
"Therefore everyone who hears these words of mine and puts them into practice is like a wise man who built his house on the rock. [25] The rain came down, the streams rose, and the winds blew

and beat against that house; yet it did not fall, because it had its foundation on the rock. [26] But everyone who hears these words of mine and does not put them into practice is like a foolish man who built his house on sand. [27] The rain came down, the streams rose, and the winds blew and beat against that house, and it fell with a great crash."

When we practice the principles of God, we reap the benefits of His promises. Successfully passing a category 2 storm always leads to promotion and increased blessings. Joseph, the Israelite, was later promoted second in authority from the Egyptian Pharaoh. Daniel survived the lion's den untouched and prospered under King Darius' reign. Job's latter days were more prosperous than his former, according to scripture. God gave him twice as much as he had before. This type of storm wouldn't whirl into our lives if we didn't have the ability to pass the test. We must remember to apply what we've learned. And stand firm on the word of God when the time for testing arises.

CHAPTER 4

Category 3 Storm:

- SELF-DESTRUCTION -
Saul's inner turmoil

- SELF-DESTRUCTION -

So far, we've explored two storm categories. A category 1 storm comes when we've been disobedient to God. So, when it rages, we should stop throwing our hands in the air and asking, "Why me?" Instead we should say, "Because of me." The purpose of this storm is to bring judgment.

On the other hand, a category 2 storm comes into our lives because of our level of spiritual maturity. It strengthens our foundation. The devil is allowed to test the faith-building word that God sows into our lives. We have enough strength, perseverance, and scripture in us to make it through this storm victoriously. Otherwise, it wouldn't rage.

Now, let's examine the nature of a category 3 storm. We don't ever want to find ourselves whirling through this type of disaster. Avoid them at all cost, because it is the most difficult storm to escape. It starts in the human mind.

1 Samuel 18:6-9 (NIV)
When the men were returning home after David

had killed the Philistine, the women came out from all the towns of Israel to meet King Saul with singing and dancing, with joyful songs and with tambourines and lutes. [7] As they danced, they sang: "Saul has slain his thousands, and David his tens of thousands." [8] Saul was very angry; this refrain galled him. "They have credited David with tens of thousands," he thought, "but me with only thousands. What more can he get but the kingdom?" [9] And from that time on Saul kept a jealous eye on David.

This particular Old Testament Bible account of Saul's inner turmoil occurred immediately after David conquered the Philistine giant named Goliath. As the combat soldiers returned from the battlefield, the Israelite women raced into the streets singing in celebration of the victory. But Saul was poorly affected and angered by the lyrics of their song. Saul focused on the fact that David was accredited for killing more Philistines than himself. David didn't do anything to Saul, but something as insignificant as a hymn ignited the beginning of Saul's internal storm.

> **We don't ever want to find ourselves whirling through this type of disaster.**

We should never allow praises given to others to

upset us, even if someone is being applauded for something they did not honestly accomplish. Get over it, quickly!

Saul, the King of Israel allowed a seed of anger to take root in his mind. Saul's assignment as King of Israel began with fear and personal insecurities. He entertained the thought that his own people recognized David to be a mightier warrior than himself. Unfortunately, Saul's outlook was distorted and based on misconstrued conceptions. Negative feelings, more often than not, spiral into evil imaginations. Saul's emotions kicked in. Instead of getting angry with the female praise singers, which would have also been unacceptable, but more understandable, he resented David. We have to understand that a category 3 storm seldom has anything to do with rationale thinking.

The pressure and force of Saul's storm began spiraling within. His battle raged within his own mind. He started having a disgruntled conversation with himself. Saul's conversation wasn't based on rationale thinking;

> **A category 3 storm seldom has anything to do with rationale thinking.**

He harbored hatred based on make-believe thoughts that ruled his imagination.

Unfortunately, many people do the same thing today. Without any hard evidence, just circumstantial undeveloped thoughts, they formulate strong views and respond to what they've imagined. Resentment and jealousy are powerfully destructive. As a result, countries go to war; spouses divorce, friends fight, and legalists battle businesses in court. Some disputes and differences of opinion are difficult to resolve, especially when multiple entities complicate solutions with personal interests. On the other hand, many fictional accounts of offense come from within – they take root in the imagination. As a result, many people are unable to conclude easy-to-solve problems, because they exaggerate circumstances and convince themselves to give in to negative thoughts. Once this happens, insight, apology, and reason are unable to reconcile even the most simplistic disputes. This is because the battle is actually raging internally.

This is another storm that doesn't come from the devil – we cause it ourselves. King Saul opened the door to an evil spirit because he refused to rid himself of resentment. The bottom line is this, Saul ended up fighting demons, because he didn't like the words to a song. Could it be because that particular song stirred Saul's longtime fears and insecurities of David's anticipated rule as King of Israel?

> **We're challenged to forgive even when we've been directly targeted or attacked, including after we've done our best.**

As a pastor, I realize leaders are often exposed to experiences that test our ability to not hold grudges. We're challenged to forgive even when we've been directly targeted or attacked, including after we've done our best.

I recall experiencing a hurtful situation with a former member of our local assembly. For the purpose of this scenario, let's call him Bob. I knew Bob for many years. He served faithfully when God birthed our ministry. Together, we shared a strong sense of excitement about the vision. We became friends.

We spent many hours together working around the

church and often fellowshipping on a personal basis outside of the ministry. I remember us discussing future possibilities, goals, and expectations. But Bob was convinced that I made promises about his future role as the ministry flourished. I accept some responsibility for his expectations. However, as our church grew, I witnessed some spiritual shortcomings in Bob's life that demanded attention.

I met with Bob and expressed my concerns. We failed to come to an understanding and Bob rejected change. If I continued to overlook his spiritual weakness, matters would have only gotten worse. So, I began to make decisions that prevented Bob from participating in ministry activities. I based my pastoral discretion on the best course of action to insure Bob's continued spiritual growth.

Resentment started brewing in Bob's mind. It seemed as though he viewed my guidance as an attack, no matter how gently I presented it. His attitude toward me changed. And our friendship progressively faded.

He refused to speak to me about his feelings,

instead he harbored bitterness inwardly. Upon noticing the dynamics of our relationship worsen, I requested several meetings attempting to resuscitate his spiritual health and our relationship. I explained how his attitude would produce unwanted spiritual implications. I expressed needed corrections, hoping to advance him into active ministry involvement. We both walked away from each meeting with an uncomfortable sensation knowing we hadn't gained an understanding.

A category 3 storm was brewing inside Bob's mind. He distanced himself from me, convinced that I was unfair, particularly towards him. Bob began to spread his perspective throughout the church. Members approached me with their concerns. Shortly after, relinquished his church membership. He said he couldn't be a part of a ministry where he perceived the leader had no integrity. What was going on in Bob's mind? I may never know.

Nonetheless, his perception of my integrity planted a potent seed of resentment in me. I refused to believe that anyone on this planet could honestly believe something like this, about totally innocent me. So, I thought. But nobody's perfect. Sincerely, I felt like I was a great guy and that he was obviously blinded by deception. "How could he not see my true motives," I thought to myself? Bob was special to me, but in his anger he overlooked my intentions. He only focused on what he perceived as my unfair actions. Here's the truth, it was difficult adjusting to the idea of being misinterpreted.

I began to notice that whenever I thought about Bob, I would get angry. Bob's category 3 storm started shifting in my direction. I instantly began to open my mouth and say, "Father, God, I forgive Bob." I sincerely asked God to bless him and his family. I did this almost daily for several weeks. I knew that my initial reaction of anger and unforgiveness would strengthen this storm. I also realized the goal of this storm was to destroy me, not just Bob. I also asked God to forgive me. Afterward, I asked Bob's forgiveness, in hopes that we would both be healed. As of today, Bob and I have not reconciled our differences. Thanks to God, I have forgiven him, released my resentment, and moved on.

It appears that Satan gained a victory. Bob and I both walked away losers in this case – our godly relationship has not been restored. A category 3 storm came and blew apart what God put together. Who knows what great things we could have accomplished had we not entertained resentful thoughts.

I pray that others don't fall victim to a category 3 storm. When people hurt us, and they will, we should be quick to forgive – even if wrongdoers haven't asked for forgiveness.

Remember Jesus' words, *"For if you forgive men when they sin against you, your heavenly Father will also forgive you. But if you do not forgive men their sins, your Father will not forgive your sins"* **Matthew 6:14-15.** We can't allow mind-boggling thoughts, whether based on facts or misconceptions, to mislead us into this type of storm. Rarely do people come out of a category 3 storm, especially without permanent damage.

This happens to church folks daily. Just because we have the gifts of the spirit working in us, does not exempt us from this

> **Just because we have the gifts of the spirit working in us, does not exempt us from this type of storm.**

This particular storm is more intense than external ones.

type of storm. The bible says Saul continued to prophesy, but he harbored resentment. David seemed clueless. Initially, he wasn't even aware that Saul was angry with him, and certainly David didn't know why. David didn't know that a storm was raging in Saul's mind. This particular storm is more intense than external ones. And it happens all the time. Stop reading for a moment and reflect. Within seconds, we're able to reminisce about people holding grudges and negative attitudes toward others.

This even happens in the church. Some Christians are clueless as to why others avoid speaking, and why they squint evil eyes, and turn cold shoulders. Offense spreads when one person offends another with cruel or even unintentional gestures, often because people feel ignored or misunderstood. Afterward, resentment invades our thought-life and cause storm-like residuals. It's best to kindly approach people when we feel offended, because short talks often diffuse escalating situations.

Otherwise, easy-to-solve offenses tend to lend this response, "I didn't do anything to them, why are they acting like that?" It's because a category 3 storm is beating against their faith – stand strong with a forgiving heart. Otherwise, the same storm their experiencing will shift in our direction, and others will start asking the same questions about us.

The first characteristic of a category 3 storm starts when an evil thought is presented to us. At this point, we have an opportunity to accept or reject negativity. The bible advises us to cast down thoughts that war against God's word.

Secondly, if we don't reject evil thoughts, we'll entertain them. People who entertain and contemplate evil thoughts magnify negative situations. Victims of a category 3 storm multiply harmful thoughts and cause scenarios to appear worse than they actually are.

The third step of a category 3 storm is when people meditate on negativity. "I can't believe they did that to me!" The only thing category 3 victims seem to think about is how wrong others did them. It seems to be their prevailing thought of the day. "They did me wrong," or "If you wrong me once, shame on you, if your wrong me twice, shame on me." The shame is actually contemplating how others hurt us, and limiting our tolerance of forgiving others.

> **Meditation is more powerful than most people think.**

Meditation is more powerful than most people think, because we ultimately become what we believe. When we meditate, we crossover into believing the things we're submitting ourselves to. We think, believe, and then become – this is how the human psyche is designed. Meditation is powerful, and it can be used for good or evil. If we're not careful, we'll start believing lies, as opposed to taking time to discern truth. Meditation leads to consumption. So, meditate on God's word, not current gossip or perceived mistreatment. When we continuously entertain evil thoughts they start controlling us. Instead, we should allow the word of God to consume our thought-life. Imagine the endless potential.

Suggestive thoughts are also powerful, especially

when entertained by negative thinkers. "Why can't I meet with the pastor, he must have his favorites?" Or a common saying is, "Who does she think she is? I'll just go to another

Running from church to church will not eliminate storms.

church!" Running from church to church will not eliminate storms. In fact, it'll take us from bad storms to even worse ones. It may seem difficult, but we can escape a category 3 storm.

Genesis 4:2-10 (NIV)

Later she gave birth to his brother Abel. Now Abel kept flocks, and Cain worked the soil. [3] In the course of time Cain brought some of the fruits of the soil as an offering to the Lord. [4] But Abel brought fat portions from some of the firstborn of his flock. The Lord looked with favor on Abel and his offering, [5] but on Cain and his offering he did not look with favor. So Cain was very angry, and his face was downcast. [6] Then the Lord said to Cain, "Why are you angry? Why is your face downcast? [7] If you do what is right, will you not be accepted? But if you do not do what is right, sin is crouching at your door; it desires to have you, but you must master it." [8] Now Cain said to his brother Abel, "Let's go out to the field." And while they were in the field, Cain attacked his brother Abel and killed him. [9] Then the Lord said to Cain,

"Where is your brother Abel?" "I don't know," he replied. "Am I my brother's keeper?" [10] The Lord said, "What have you done? Listen! Your brother's blood cries out to me from the ground.

Adam's son, Cain, got upset when God didn't accept his offering. Cain sincerely thought that God loved Abel more, even though we know that God does not show favoritism. Cain took his anger out on his brother Abel and killed him. There is no record of Abel gloating or taunting his brother. In fact, he did not do anything that warranted his murder. When we're in a category 3 storm, even God Himself can speak, but we won't listen. This is because victims of this type of storm create their own realities. That's why this storm is the worse – it turns our minds into battlefields. But if we listen and meditate on the word of God we can come out of this storm, too.

People in a category 3 storm will think of us as an enemy if we try to help them. They'll accuse us of taking sides, especially if we try to help them accept their own faults. They'll even stop communicating with us if we try to reason with them or make peace. They don't accept apologies well, if at all. And they spread disease and destruction.

The only way out of this storm is for us to open our mouths and confess forgiveness. This storm often becomes more intense than others. Sometimes it takes months to break through the eye of a category 3 storm. The human mind and spirit have to come into agreement in order to escape complete disaster. Here's a simple warning, when we reject truth, we make ourselves subject to lies.

1 Kings 22:21-22 (NIV)

Finally, a spirit came forward, stood before the Lord and said, 'I will entice him.' [22] 'By what means?' the Lord asked." 'I will go out and be a lying spirit in the mouths of all his prophets,' he said." 'You will succeed in enticing him,' said the Lord. 'Go and do it.'

When we're in a category 3 storm, it's imperative that we watch who we communicate with. People only tell us what they think we prefer hearing after they've been exposed to our wound-infected attitude. "You're right," is what they'll usually say, because most people don't like fighting and arguing, especially when negativity prevents others from listening. It's a whirlwind of deception, because people trapped in this storm generally connect to lies and distance themselves from truth. "I should start my own church," and "People are only here because of..." What about, "I don't need them anyway" and "I don't want to talk about it now!" Let's identify a few other commonly used statements and questions people in this storm make. "What makes you think you're always right," and "I'm saved, I hear from God, too, right?"

Get over it

These are some of the thoughts category 3 storm victims think. Let's pause and examine our thoughts. I understand what it feels like to get hurt unexpectedly, but let it go. Get over it! Many non-believers have endured worse treatment than some Christians, and some of them have done so more honorably. We're forgiven, so, it's imperative that we practice forgiveness.

Genesis 4:14 (NIV)
Today you are driving me from the land, and I will be hidden from your presence; I will be a restless wanderer on the earth, and whoever finds me will kill me."

This is what happens when we reject the truth of God's word – we are removed from His presence. His word is saying forgive, but when our actions are displaying unforgiveness we're warring against Him. Christians should embrace the heart of David,

"God, don't take your spirit from me." Young David continuously forgave King Saul, even though Saul pur-posed in his heart to kill him. Now, compare David's

> **Don't submit to carnal aspirations.**

attitude to modern day Church folks. We have a difficult time forgiving minor disputes, opposing opinions, silent treatments, and other offenses that aren't nearly life threatening. The truth is simple, we must learn to forgive.

Don't submit to carnal aspirations. Some people wander aimlessly from church to church, job to job, friend to friend, and relationship to relation-ship. This is a sign of people who place their confidence in men as opposed to God. Wherever we go and with whomever we're with, we'll have no peace in the midst of this storm. This is what happens when we refuse to forgive. We become wanderers caught in the turmoil of self-deception and bitterness.

What is the purpose of a category 3 storm? That answer is simple – it's self-destruction. When Saul refused to forgive, after years of opportunity collapsed, his life concluded in an episode of suicide. He fell onto his spear to prevent his enemies from killing him in battle.

> **The purpose of a category 3 storm is self-destruction.**

If we reject truth the outcome will not be good. Some people, like Saul, think they can escape the consequences of unforgiveness. So, when others attempt to connect, negative thinkers reply with curt and sarcastic remarks, "I'm good," or "I'm fine." Afterward, they often justify their responses by saying, "They were just speaking to me to prove a point, so, I don't have anything to say to them!" A rose remains beautiful days after being clipped from its roots. Initially, it appears as though clipped roses can live forever. Women cherish them. But regardless of how well we care for a clipped rose, its ultimate fate is death. Some people think, "Nothing has happened to me yet." Understand that we cannot escape sin's penalty.

Some people are great when it comes to relating with others, even amid contention. They hide behind bright smiles and firm hand shakes. Be advised that a category 3 storm isn't limited to

- Saul's inner turmoil -

> **If we don't learn to control our thought-life, we will blow many situations out of control.**

negative relationships. If we don't learn to control our thought-life, we will blow all types of situations out off proportion. Even small cuts can turn into severe infections. Category 3 storm victims are people who find themselves rubbing an itchy bump on their chest, afterward wondering, "Maybe I need to go to the doctor?" The mind creates various realities based on fear or faith. As a result, the mind makes people think a mosquito bite is a cancerous lump or a hand full of vegetable seeds is a flourishing garden. Our thought-life is dictated by fear or faith.

What's the driving force behind your actions? We're able to determine the answer to this question by examining the type of thoughts that dominate our lives. This storm affects people in various ways, but this chapter deals largely with relationships, because that's where this storm usually starts.

Proverbs 18:19 (NIV)
An offended brother is more unyielding than a

fortified city, and disputes are like the barred gates of a citadel.

It's not a pretty site to see people in a category 3 storm state. Marriages are particularly vulnerable during this storm. Often, the root of bitter divorces can be traced to gross misunderstanding of actions and motives. Constructive communication is critical. Internal storms often separate what God has joined together. Husbands, Christ encourage us to love our wives. Therefore, I passionately teach listeners about the love of God. Disastrous storms are spiraling out of control in countless marriages, even in Christian circles.

II Corinthians 10:5 (NIV)
We demolish arguments and every pretension that sets itself up against the knowledge of God, and we take captive every thought to make it obedient to Christ.

Remember, the only way out of this storm is for us to open our mouths in forgiveness and arrest our thought-life. No one else can do this for us. Although negative thoughts tend to leap into our minds, we have to keep bringing them into captivity. For example, start by repeating this, "Lord, I forgive."

Mark 11:25 (NIV)
And when you stand praying, if you hold anything against anyone, forgive him, so that your Father in heaven may forgive you your sins."

After we arrest our negative thoughts, we must forgive. Forgiveness is critical in our Christian walk. If we fail to forgive others, the Bible says, God will refuse to forgive us. Finally, the only way to avoid this storm is by taking control of our thoughts. We take control of our thoughts by renewing our mind with the word of God.

Philippians 4:8 (NIV)
And the peace of God, which transcends all understanding, will guard your hearts and your minds in Christ Jesus. [8] Finally, brothers, whatever is true, whatever is noble, whatever is right, whatever is pure, whatever is lovely, whatever is admirable--if anything is excellent or praiseworthy--think about such things.

CHAPTER 5

Category 4 Storm:

- POISONOUS -
*Herod's pride and
Nebuchadnezzar's idols*

- POISONOUS -

Most of us have experienced times in life when situations seem perfect. Our plans keep producing great successes. Our hard work is paying high dividends. And it seems everyone is patting us on the back with praise. "You're such a blessing, if it weren't for you, this would not have gotten done!" Those words are probably ringing in our ears, along with, "Thanks, you're the best!" This is how people around us reinforce encouragement. They shower us with accolades and sometimes even make us feel like we can move mountains with our physical strength.

Quite often when we're strolling along life's successes, we're tempted to pat ourselves on the back for daily accomplishments. Although this season makes us feel really good about ourselves, we must remain prayerful and humble. It's imperative that we remained focused on Christ, who is the reason why all things work together for our good.

How we respond to compliments and proud pats on the back will determine our future. The right response will lead to promotion, but the wrong reaction can lead to a category 4 storm.

A category 4 storm is driven by pride. Pride defined by Webster is "an overly high opinion of one-self; exaggerated self-esteem, conceit; or an

> **A category 4 storm is driven by pride.**

excessive belief in ones own self-worth." Secular psychologists and professional counselors encourage clients to build their self-esteem. In our progressive society, it's common for people to rely on the confidence of their own abilities. This self-help theory appears logical, but the Bible teaches us to esteem others higher than ourselves, and to glorify God for our individual successes.

This is a critically complicated issue, because it's easy to take credit for our individual endeavors when God appears absent. Recognizing that we are vulnerable, and understanding that God is responsible for our abilities, is how we can elimi-nates pride. Give this school of theology some thought. Otherwise, our very opinions of ourselves will displease the creator.

Here is God's opinion of pride: *"There are six*

things the LORD hates, seven that are detestable to him: haughty eyes **(Proverbs 6:16-17).** Notice, the first on the list of seven displeasures is proud eyes.

Pride is the very reason Satan is eternally banished from heaven.

Pride is the very reason Satan is eternally banished from heaven. The devil became so impressed with himself that he thought he should be exalted or esteemed above God. Workers resign, spouses divorce, and churchgoers change congregations all too often, because they think they're deserving of higher positions. The Bible says promotion comes from God. If we believe the Bible, and have faith in God, then why do we depend on our supervisors, spouses, and pastors instead of praying for expected outcomes? Perhaps we demand quick responses from others because prayer requires patience and humility.

Notice Satan's approach. During Christ's wilderness experience, Satan, possessed with pride, tempted the Son of God to kneel and worship him.

> **Satan will try to persuade us to exaggerate our self-worth.**

Imagine his audacity. How arrogant can one be to ask the creator to worship creation Satan's pride caused a storm that he couldn't reverse. During a war in heaven, angels cast out the devil, and sentenced him to time on earth to await eternal damnation. Satan's pride resulted in eternal condemnation for a third of heaven's angels who suffered the same penalty. Now, he attempts to persuade Christians with pride, much like he convinced fallen angels to exaggerate their self-worth.

We often think, "Satan is ignorant." Is he really? Ignorance means unlearned. The Bible says the devil is beguiling. He is a charmer who artfully deceives his victims. In fact, Satan influenced a host of angels to forsake eternity in paradise, while they were yet in God's presence. Pride is a destructive force that God will not tolerate in His kingdom.

Storms driven by pride are generally severe. They often result in massive loss. Let's look at a different dimension of a category 4 storm found in the book of Daniel.

Daniel 4:28-37 (NIV)

All this happened to King Nebuchadnezzar. [29] Twelve months later, as the king was walking on the roof of the royal palace of Babylon, [30] he said, "Is not this the great Babylon I have built as the royal residence, by my mighty power and for the glory of my majesty?" [31] The words were still on his lips when a voice came from heaven, "This is what is decreed for you, King Nebuchadnezzar: Your royal authority has been taken from you. [32] You will be driven away from people and will live with the wild animals; you will eat grass like cattle. Seven times will pass by for you until you acknowledge that the Most High is sovereign over the kingdoms of men and gives them to anyone he wishes." [33] Immediately what had been said about Nebuchadnezzar was fulfilled. He was driven away from people and ate grass like cattle. His body was drenched with the dew of heaven until his hair grew like the feathers of an eagle and his nails like the claws of a bird. [34] At the end of that time, I, Nebuchadnezzar, raised my eyes toward heaven, and my sanity was restored. Then I praised the Most High; I honored and glorified him who lives forever. His dominion is an eternal dominion; his kingdom endures from generation to generation. [35] All the peoples of the earth are regarded as nothing. He does as he pleases with the powers of heaven and the peoples of the earth. No one can hold back his hand or say to him: "What have you done?" [36]   At the same time that my sanity was restored, my honor and splendor were returned to me for the glory of my kingdom. My advisers and nobles sought me out, and I was restored to my throne and became even greater than before. [37] Now I, Nebuchadnezzar, praise and exalt and glorify the King of heaven, because everything he does is right and all his ways are just. And those who walk in pride he is able to humble.

God used King Nebuchadnezzar to execute judgment against the children of Israel.   He allowed the kingdom of Babylon to prosper under Nebuchadnezzar's reign, because the prosperity of Babylon resulted in the preservation of Israel. Israel is God's chosen people.   And ultimately, God is responsible for the greatness of the kingdom, not Nebuchadnezzar.

Imagine the masses surrounding Nebuchadnezzar's throne, constantly praising him for the magnificent kingdom he built.   They were probably very genuine in their flattery.   According to scripture, they believed that the greatness of Babylon was due to the strength and wisdom of Nebuchadnezzar.

It wasn't long before King Nebuchadnezzar started

embellishing his confidence based on their kind words. When in fact, compliments should merely confirm that perhaps we're doing something good. It's a simple way of rewarding good works. But when we allow compliments to feed our ego, we're headed in the wrong direction. Nebuchadnezzar became convinced that he was the source of Babylon's greatness. **Daniel 4:30 (NIV)** "Is not this the great Babylon *I* have built as the royal residence, by *my* mighty power and for the glory of *my* majesty," Nebuchadnezzar asked?

God responded to Nebuchadnezzar's pride immediately. The Bible says he was still speaking when God severely reprimanded him. What's the big deal if someone wants to take credit for something they've accomplished? Why is God so angered by what appears to be very innocent behavior on our part? God knows that pride will cause us to believe that we are self-reliant, and that we don't need to depend on Him. When in reality we need God more than we can ever imagine.

> **We need God more than we can ever imagine.**

Pride causes us to see ourselves as the ultimate

source. It makes us feel and think we have all the needed answers. It unconscientiously causes us to worship our own talents, strengths, and abilities. Instead, all glory belongs to God, and he's the only One deserving of our worship. Pride can also expose others to harm, because without careful consideration, listeners will look to us for life's answers prior to consulting God.

God has clearly stated: **Exodus 20:3-5 (NIV)** *"You shall have no other gods before me. [4] "You shall not make for yourself an idol in the form of anything in heaven above or on the earth beneath or in the waters below. [5] You shall not bow down to them or worship them; for I, the Lord your God, am a jealous God, punishing the children for the sin of the fathers to the third and fourth genera-tion of those who hate me.*

Whenever we erect idols, God's objective is to bring them down, even if the idols are ourselves or others. This category 4 storm resulted in Nebu-chadnezzar's insanity. Insanity is an appropriate description for anyone who takes credit for what God does, even if God uses us to do it.

Eating grass like animals caused others to view Nebuchadnezzar like a public spectacle. The royal king of Babylon was abased to eating wild grass with field animals. He was totally stripped of his position – no status and no honor. Nebuchadnezzar was reduced to a mad man in the presence of those who once swelled his heart with flattery. There are

> **There are two quick solutions for pride, we can humble ourselves or allow God to humble us.**

two quick solutions for pride, we can humble ourselves or allow God to humble us. It's less troublesome if we learn to humble ourselves.

Nebuchadnezzar did not have anyone to blame. He worshiped his accomplishments instead of God. We initiate this storm, Satan is merely an influence. This type of behavior is totally avoidable!

If we find ourselves trapped in a category 4 storm, it's best for us to humble ourselves and repent. Remember, God hates pride. To prevent the sweltering stench of pride, we should always worship and praise the creator for our successes.

The debilitating and humiliating effect of this storm caused Nebuchadnezzar to realize that God exalted him to his previous status. God also humbled him. Nebuchadnezzar concluded that he wasn't such a "hot shot" after all. Ultimately, he realized God worked through him and caused greatness throughout the kingdom.

A category 4 storm will last until we either repent or perish, according to **Daniel 4:36-37 (NIV).** As a result of Nebuchadnezzar repenting, God quickly restored everything he lost. In fact, the Bible says Nebuchadnezzar became greater than he was before. The alternative to repentance in a category 4 storm is destruction, according to this New Testament example in the book of Acts.

Acts 12:21-23 (NIV)
On the appointed day Herod, wearing his royal robes, sat on his throne and delivered a public address to the people. [22] They shouted, "This is the voice of a god, not of a man." [23] Immediately, because Herod did not give praise to God, an angel of the Lord struck him down, and he was eaten by worms and died.

There are possibly other judgments that fall between the boundaries of this Old Testament example of restoration and Herod's New Testament example of perishing. However, why would a Christian risk suffering the kind of judgment that comes from God's hatred of pride? We must guard ourselves against this satanic influence. Its devastating effects should encourage us to examine ourselves routinely.

As a pastor, supported by the kind deeds and complimenting voices of countless parishioners, I constantly guard myself from the spirit of pride. After Christ anoints my Sunday teachings, members of the congregation compliment me for God's awesomeness. "You are such a blessing," and "Your message was incredible – I needed that!" Although the compliments are appreciated, it's situations like these that make me vulnerable to Satan's scheme.

It's tempting to take credit for touching the lives of thousands of listeners, but I've learned to redirect their focus and give God glory. Every message I teach is given to me by the Holy Spirit. The revelation of God's word, and the ability to effectively communicate such knowledge to His people, are both gifts from Him.

I recall over a decade ago when the mere thought of public speaking petrified me to chills. Speeches and lectures were not my forte. My communication skills were minimal. I had feelings of inadequacy and great fear. I often concerned myself with the idea of listeners being more knowledgeable than myself. While speaking, the edges of my mouth dried rapidly creating an unusual discomfort – I experienced instant dehydration. My voice quivered and I spoke with uncertain tones.

So, why would God call a 34-year-old business professional and seemingly inadequate public speaker to pastor a church? October 1990, Joyce and I followed God's instructions and started what newspaper reporters have labeled as one of the fastest growing ministries in our city.

Didn't God realize what this would require? Absolutely, He did! And He makes all things possible when we solely rely on him. To my great amazement, when I began to pastor and teach the word of God, His power and anointing served as guides to my lips. While teaching, the Holy Spirit whispers divine revelation to me. God uses the words flowing from my mouth to bless me

> **It's tempting to take credit for touching the lives of thousands of listeners.**

as well as others. To include, all fear is gone! In fact, I teach with such boldness that I am often startled by what comes out of my mouth. I'm continuously giving God thanks for using me as a willing vessel.

> **Apostle Paul said it best, "But by the grace of God I am what I am."**
> **As long as we live according to this principle, we can avoid a category 4 storm.**

Kind-hearted parishioners seem to expect me to say, "thank you" for their complimentary remarks. But I can't, because all praises belong to God. Some even reply, "Well, you're the vessel God is using and I thank God for you." I immediately respond with humility, "Praise God." Always remembering where the Lord has brought me from. I will always accredit God for everything good He enables me to produce.

Our ministry has been able to implement productive programs that are highly visible in our region. We operate a K-9 school, employment and computer training courses, transitional housing, a food bank, and other outreach programs. Local residents politely compliment me by saying, "You're doing a great job, Pastor Oliver!" I'm repetitive at saying, "It's not me. God is blessing us." Every blessing people see, hear, or read about our church is from God.

Perhaps some people think my logic of refusing to take credit is going overboard, but I'm not. We were born to give God glory. It's God's desire that when people learn of Christians, they'll desire to know Him. Apostle Paul said it best, *"But by the grace of God I am what I am, (1 Corinthians 15:10).* As long as we live according to this principle, we can avoid a category 4 storm.

CHAPTER 6

-WHO'S IN YOUR BOAT?-
Storm starters are trouble makers

-WHO'S IN YOUR BOAT?-

W ho are storm starters and trouble makers? Most often, these are people who are presently going through one of the four storms we've mentioned. They cause us to experience the affect of their consequences when we welcome them in our lives. They cause noticeable chaos. And sometimes innocent bystanders are unaware of disturbances others bring into their lives. The sailors at Joppa welcomed Jonah aboard their ship after he paid his fare. Seems like the polite and professional thing to do. They later learned the importance of not doing business with people they knew nothing about. The ship is comparable to our lives in this passage of scripture – we decide what cargo we choose to carry. It's important not to allow others to load seeds of disobedience and rebellion into our ship.

Jonah 1:1-12 (NIV)
The word of the Lord came to Jonah son of Amittai: [2] "Go to the great city of Nineveh and preach against it, because its wickedness has come up before me." [3] But Jonah ran away from the Lord and headed for Tarshish. He went down to Joppa, where he found a ship bound for that port. After paying the fare, he went aboard and sailed

for Tarshish to flee from the Lord. [4] Then the Lord sent a great wind on the sea, and such a violent storm arose that the ship threatened to break up. [5] All the sailors were afraid and each cried out to his own god. And they threw the cargo into the sea to lighten the ship. But Jonah had gone below deck, where he lay down and fell into a deep sleep. [6] The captain went to him and said, "How can you sleep? Get up and call on your god! Maybe he will take notice of us, and we will not perish." [7] Then the sailors said to each other, "Come, let us cast lots to find out who is responsible for this calamity." They cast lots and the lot fell on Jonah. [8] So they asked him, "Tell us, who is responsible for making all this trouble for us? What do you do? Where do you come from? What is your country? From what people are you?" [9] He answered, "I am a Hebrew and I worship the Lord, the God of heaven, who made the sea and the land." [10] This terrified them and they asked, "What have you done?" (They knew he was running away from the Lord, because he had already told them so.) [11] The sea was getting rougher and rougher. So they asked him, "What should we do to you to make the sea calm down for us?" [12] "Pick me up and throw me into the sea," he replied, "and it will become calm. I know that it is my fault that this great storm has come upon you."

The men on the boat were not acquainted with Jonah when they obliged him to come abroad. That's how most people are; it's the norm. Instead of evaluating strangers before allowing them in our

Have you ever allowed the wrong person in your inner-circle?

lives, we welcome foreign ideas and strange concepts. Diversity is important. We teach our congregation to value it. On the other hand, all too often, Christians welcome views that directly conflict with the word of God. We shouldn't allow just anyone to develop a relationship with us. Just because someone pays for our breakfast, lunch, or dinner does not qualify them to come aboard our ship. It's important to examine the lives of people on our ships before it's too late. Have you ever allowed the wrong person in your inner-circle? Jonah didn't care about the trouble he caused in the lives of others. He was identical to modern day trouble-makers who secretly cause calamity, and then quickly stand back and watch catastrophe take place.

When people attempt to develop relationship with us, we should ask important questions. Inquire about their intentions without seeming judgmental and withdrawn. If we allow rebellious people in our lives, we'll find ourselves wading through storms with them.

After the winds began to blow fiercely, the men on the ship questioned Jonah. Once this storm is raging, it's risky, and often too late to easily solve the problem. What is your occupation, where are you from, and what God do you serve? These are a few questions they asked Jonah, and we should ask others the same. After we've assessed various situations, then we're able to make educated decisions about people who try to come into our lives.

Unfortunately, the only way to rid ourselves of undeserved storms is to throw sinful people overboard. It may sound harsh to some Christians, but we must rid ourselves of rebellious people at all cost. When we are in close fellowship with rebellious people, their behavior will transfer into our lives. It's spiritual in nature. **I Corinthians 15:33** tells us that bad company corrupts good character.

> **It may sound harsh to some Christians, but we must rid ourselves of rebellious people at all cost.**

How can two people that are yoked together walk in different directions? They can't. And destroying yokes require a costly anointing. Most people aren't bold enough to tell others to get off their ship. Neither are Christians willing to toss others overboard, it's seems impolite and unprofessional. But if we're anticipating success, productivity, prosperity, good health, and long life, bad seeds must go. In

> **There are some people we are going to have to forcefully kick off our ship.**

fact, we're better off not allowing storm starters and trouble makers to come into our lives.

There are some people we are going to have to forcefully kick off our ship. These are the people that keep calling us at work, home, and on our cellular phones after we've ask them to stop. They refuse to live according to the word of God and have no intentions on changing. They keep coming around after we've severed the relationship. Throw them overboard, quickly! Other than spouses, there are no exceptions for people possessing the potential of being thrown out of our ships. Family members, friends, co-workers, and church members sometimes need to be tossed overboard. Yes, even family and church members.

The Bible teaches us that churches contain goats,

wolves, and sheep. Sheep follow shepherds, but goats go against the grain. And if unattended, wolves will destroy entire herds of sheep. Have you ever seen how one person can negatively affect an entire church? Wolves attacking and eating sheep is a grueling visual of how rebellion eats away at other people's good intentions. If we find ourselves connected to a person who is in a category 1 storm, where they are rebellious, disobedient, and sinful, we need to remove them from our lives without considering other options.

Satan's easiest entry into lives is through the people we're already close to. It's difficult to accept, but it's the truth. Most of the greatest storms I've experienced in ministry have started with people in my inner circle. Particularly, relationships in a category 2 storm are critical, because this storm enters our lives for testing and promotion. If those close to us don't understand the nature of this storm, they're prone to make our experience even more miserable.

> **Sheep follow shepherds, but goats go against the grain. And if unattended, wolves will destroy entire herds of sheep.**

The weakest link in our inner-circle will often be responsible for initiating our storm. After someone betrays or hurts us, we often get offended. And if we aren't careful it's easy to transition from the benefits that follow a category 2 storm into the penalty of a category 3 storm. Don't go from promotion status to destruction. We shouldn't be paranoid of our friends - just prayerful and alert.

During a category 2 storm, others will think we're going through difficult times resulting from sin. Even inner-circle friends will add insult to injury by questioning our relationship with God. Job's friends and wife questioned his faith when he reached his lowest point.

Job 4:3-8 (NIV)
Think how you have instructed many, how you have strengthened feeble hands. [4] Your words have supported those who stumbled; you have strengthened faltering knees. [5] But now trouble comes to you, and you are discouraged; it strikes you, and you are dismayed. [6] Should not your piety be your confidence and your blameless ways your hope? [7] "Consider now: Who, being inno-cent, has ever perished? Where were the upright ever destroyed? [8] As I have observed, those who plow evil and those who sow trouble reap it.

With friends like these who needs enemies, huh? Now, imagine going through life's greatest storm, and our closest friends say, "Those who sow trouble reap trouble." They were actually judging Job and accusing him of wrongdoing, even though God called him blameless and upright. If we're hanging with the wrong group of people, during troublesome times, they will deflate air out of our spiritual balloons. Focused Christians surround themselves with people who speak the word of God – those who encourage rather than judge our lives.

Finally, if we are in relationship with a person going through a category 3 storm, we'd better make an "about face" and start sprinting quickly! Run! These people will harm us! They are not pleasant to be around. They need deliverance, not counseling. They need prayer, not understanding. Although they'll desire to be heard, what they have to say is not worth listening

Run! These people will harm us! They are not pleasant to be around. They need deliverance, not counseling. They need prayer, not understanding.

to. Category 3 storm vic-
tims are so miserable that
they only find pleasure
when they're lashing out at
others. Sometimes they
seem to be the most pleasant and adorable people.
But once they've been
wounded they spit venom
and spread infectious poi-
son.

> **Sometimes they seem to be the most pleasant and adorable people. But once they've been wounded they spit venom and spread infectious poison.**

Most often than not, they seem to have good intentions. But once we've gotten close enough to gain a nearby glance and lend a listening ear, they bite us. However, our prayers are powerful, and always prove to be more worthwhile for these particular storm victims. In addition, listening to complaints put us at risk of becoming plagued with the same negative thought processes.

1 Samuel 18:11 (NIV)
and he hurled it, saying to himself, "I'll pin David to the wall." But David eluded him twice. And Saul cast the javelin; for he said, I will smite David even to the wall with it. And David avoided out of his presence twice.

Category 3 storm victims are like deep-black holes that suck in everything around them. They attempt to overshadow light. They aggressively pull people into their consequences, because like Satan, they want others to partake in their misery. Either we are influencing them or they are influencing us. That's why it's imperative that we know the intents, thoughts, and motives of people we allow in our lives.

- FINAL WORDS -
You have a destiny

- FINAL WORDS -

Let's revisit the boat where Jesus was found resting during the violent storm. Prior to departure, Jesus predetermined their destination.

Mark 4:35-41 (NIV)
That day when evening came, he said to his disciples, "Let us go over to the other side." [36] Leaving the crowd behind, they took him along, just as he was, in the boat. There were also other boats with him. [37] A furious squall came up, and the waves broke over the boat, so that it was nearly swamped. [38] Jesus was in the stern, sleeping on a cushion. The disciples woke him and said to him, "Teacher, don't you care if we drown?" [39] He got up, rebuked the wind and said to the waves, "Quiet! Be still!" Then the wind died down and it was completely calm. [40] He said to his disciples, "Why are you so afraid? Do you still have no faith?" [41] They were terrified and asked each other, "Who is this? Even the wind and the waves obey him!"

As Christians, we must always remember Jesus is in our boat, no matter how fierce the storm. While the waves were crashing into the wooden boat, and the disciples seemed hopelessly drenched, Jesus was awaiting the right response.

God will never leave us alone. He's present during every storm. The Lord is waiting for us to obey and speak His word. In order to place emphasis on the validity of this theory, let's take a drastic turn and consider the creation account.

> **As Christians, we must always remember Jesus is in our boat, no matter how fierce the storm.**

Genesis 1:1-2 (NIV)
In the beginning God created the heavens and the earth. [2] Now the earth was formless and empty, darkness was over the surface of the deep, and the Spirit of God was hovering over the waters.

Bible scholars say that during the creation account the earth was undergoing a turbulent time. Since the Spirit of God was not operating on the earth, everything on the planet was in total chaos and confusion. The earth was experiencing a major storm. The Bible says the "Spirit of God" was hovering over the waters. During the worse geographical turmoil in the planets history, the Spirit of God was present, but not active. The Holy Spirit anxiously awaited God's command. God spoke, sprung into action, and brought peace to a chaotic planet. When God said "Let there be," order was

> **Regardless of what kind of storm we're experiencing, we must always remember that God never forsakes His people.**

restored. God's word will eliminate every storm we encounter. And we have the assurance that He is always with us. *"Never will I leave you; never will I forsake you"* **Hebrews 13:5**. This is a reality even during our worst experiences.

It's a good thing Jesus was in the boat with the disciples. The storm was so strong that they cast hope overboard. This is the attitude many believers embrace when turbulent winds start blowing in our lives – we often lose faith. But there's another option. After panicking, the disciples turned and called on Jesus.

Regardless of what kind of storm we're experiencing, we must always remember that God never forsakes His people. The Lord is waiting for us to turn toward Him. And if we remain focused, God's word will guide us to our expected destination.

During a category 1 storm, turn to; **1 John 1:9-10 (NIV)** *If we confess our sins, he is faithful and* *just and will forgive us our sins and purify us from all unrighteousness. [10] If we claim we have not sinned, we make him out to be a liar and his word has no place in our lives.*

During a category 2 storm, turn to; **Isaiah 54:17 (NIV)** *no weapon forged against you will prevail, and you will refute every tongue that accuses you. This is the heritage of the servants of the Lord, and this is their vindication from me," declares the Lord.*

During a category 3 storm, turn to; **Philippians 4:8-9 (NIV)** *Finally, brothers, whatever is true, whatever is noble, whatever is right, whatever is pure, whatever is lovely, whatever is admirable--if anything is excellent or praiseworthy--think about such things. [9] Whatever you have learned or received or heard from me, or seen in me--put it into practice. And the God of peace will be with you.*

During a category 4 storm, turn to; **James 4:6-7 (NIV)** *But he gives us more grace. That is why Scripture says: "God opposes the proud but gives grace to the humble." [7] Submit yourselves, then, to God. Resist the devil, and he will flee from you.*

When we turn to the word, we can speak to our storms. Consider what Christ did during His storm. **Mark 4:39** He was not shaken by difficult circumstances. Instead, Jesus commanded the winds and the storm to obey him. The bible teaches us that we have the authority and power to speak to our situations.

The Holy Spirit is in position to calm our current storms, but He remains quiet until He hears us speak the word of God. Perhaps some believers are familiar with the lyrics to the song, "Somewhere over the rainbow?" Well, there's also another side of our storms. After our faith has been tested, a greater destination awaits us. Our destiny is directly affected by our level of faith.

Every storm has life altering affects. Some storms lead to devastating consequences, while others provide promotion potential. There are many possible outcomes for each storm category.

A category 1 storm results from sin, disobedience, and/or rebellion. After Jonah spent three days in torment, he repented, and his storm stopped. God gave him a second chance. Afterward, Jonah received the same instructions he initially disobeyed. In essence, when Jonah arrived at the other side of his storm, he was right back at square one. He didn't gain or lose any ground.

Jonah had to start over. He eventually obeyed God's initial instructions.

> **Some storms lead to devastating consequences, while others provide promotion potential.**

Contrary to false notions, rebellion and disobedience always has consequences. Sin does not go unnoticed before God. Although forgiven, even Christians have to cope with the consequences of their actions. For example, we see unwed mothers birthing children daily. Men and women repent of fornication, God forgives, and then newborns are still delivered. Also, we've encountered countless recovering drug addicts restart at the bottom of the economic ladder. And although God forgives cheating spouses who participate in adulterous affairs, when exposed, these marriages often end in divorce. Even after forgiveness, category 1 storm victims can anticipate suffering loss.

A category 2 storm is a result of testing because of our righteousness and spiritual maturity. This storm quite often challenges our faith to its core - we are generally pushed to our limit. Although, we can triumph victoriously, much like Job, who kept his integrity and maintained his faith in God. Even

Joseph endured persecution, slavery, and impris-
onment with faith. In addition, Daniel stepped out
of the lions den unharmed. And Jesus walked out
of the wilderness raising the dead, healing the sick,
and giving sight to the blind.

In every case, the other
side of a category 2 storm
produced promotion. Job
restored exceedingly more
than he loss. Joseph, the
Israelite, became the
equivalent of an Egyptian
prince. Daniel ruled in
Babylon. Jesus walked out

Our destiny is greater than our current destination.

the desert operating in divine authority. He conquered Satan. Persistently pressing our way
through a category 2 storm will lead to a harvest
of great reward. Our destiny is greater than our
current destination.

A category 3 storm is internal. We generate its
force and impact based on our thoughts. The devil
is not the cause of this storm, we are. This type of
storm is commonly rooted in unforgiveness, bitterness, resentment, and envy. It's generally birthed

out of negativity and laborious meditation. People experiencing this storm believe lies rather than truth. It's painfully difficult, and sometimes impossible, to convince this type of storm victim that they've been deceived.

People seldom triumph from a category 3 storm. Cain was banished from the presence of God when his internal storm caused him to murder his brother. Saul's jealously and resentment resulted in several attempted murders of David. Instead, Saul committed suicide.

Here's one category 3 storm example that ended without total loss. Envy and jealousy caused Joseph's brothers to trade him into slavery. Years later, Joseph restored his brothers with forgiveness. They are known as the twelve tribes of Israel. Their route to restoration was no easy journey – they endured a season of severe famine. But they made it to the other side.

> **How low must God allow us to go, in effort to adjust our attitudes with humility and rid us of pride?**

A category 4 storm is produced by pride. This storm

is also mind boggling and difficult to escape. Satan never repented for his pride. Although banished from heaven, he continues to rebel and refuses to humble himself before God.

The citizens of Babel felt self-motivated to make a name for themselves. Instead, they should have allowed God to make a name for them. Interesting enough, God used multiple languages to scatter mankind across the earth. He brought an end to their efforts to build a tower to heaven.

King Herod accepted praise of men and refused to give praise to God. Upon dying, his corpse was eaten by worms. This type of storm should be avoided at all cost, because judgment against pride is severe.

Nebuchadnezzar made it to the other side of his category 4 storm. After suffering insanity and living with animal-like tendencies, he finally gave God praise. It's never too late to repent and serve God. Nebuchadnezzar regained his sanity and the kingdom. The scripture also explains that he became greater after his storm.

How low must God allow us to go, in effort to adjust our attitudes with humility and rid us of pride? Pride is a stubborn spirit. It's risky and impossible trying to sail to the other side of a storm while latched to pride at the same time. Remember, strong winds will blow, but Jesus will help you arrive safely at your destiny.

CEDRIC OLIVER

The words written in this book have blessed many. Hopefully, this revelation has provided readers with valuable insight on how to navigate through spiritual storms. This is not an exhaustive commentary on storms; there's much more to learn. Hopefully readers have familiarized themselves enough to identity, avoid, or get out of spiritual storms. God's desire is to turn our hurricanes into hope. We can overcome life's crisis with the help of Christ, and experience conquests over crisis.

Pray for people who are enduring fierce storms and looking for answers to escape life's most difficult circumstances. We must make a decision to please God in everything we do, and then our category 2 storm will end in promotion. And our unproductive storms will turn into clear skies of hope.

BIBLICAL CROSS REFERENCES

Category 1: THE FUGITIVE
Jonah's disobedience and rebellion

Adam and Eve: Genesis 3
Sodom and Gomorrah : Genesis 19
Nation of Israel: Numbers 14:1-35
Blessing and Curses: Deuteronomy 28:1-68
Achan: Joshua 7
Samson: Judges 16
King Saul: 1 Samuel 13:1-14
Uzzah: 2 Samuel 6:1-7
King David: 2 Samuel 24
Ananias and Sapphira: Acts 5:1-10

Category 2: THIS IS ONLY A TEST
Job's righteousness and maturity

Joseph: Genesis 37, 38-40
Job: Job 1-2:1-10
Shadrach, Meshach, Abednego: Daniel 3
Daniel: Daniel 6
Jesus: Luke 4:1-13
Peter and Apostles: Acts 5:27-42
Stephen: Acts 6:8-15, 7:54-59
Paul: 2 Corinthians 11:23-28

Category 3: SELF-DESTRUCTION
Saul's inner turmoil

Cain: Genesis 4:1-14
Joseph's Brothers: Genesis 37:1-28
King Saul: 1 Samuel 18:5-12
Herod: Matthew 2:1-18

Category 4: POISON
Herod's Pride and
Nebuchadnezzar's Idols

Tower of Babel: Genesis 11:1-9
Satan: Ezekiel 28:11-19
Nebuchadnezzar: Dan 4:28-37
Herod: Acts 12:21-23
Paul: 2 Corinthians 12:1-9

-Index of 25 Most Commonly Asked Questions-

Chapter 3 THIS IS ONLY A TEST, Category 2

10. Ever encountered the force of a storm even after obeying God specific instructions?

11. Why am I not getting the expected results when I do the right thing?

12. So, what's the purpose of this storm?

Chapter 4 SELF-DESTRUCTION, Category 3

13. Why me?

14. What's going on in your mind?

15. I didn't do anything to them, why are they acting like that?

16. Why can't I meet with the pastor, he must have his favorites?

17. Who does she think she is?

18. What is the purpose of a category 3 storm?

Chapter 5 POISONOUS, Category 4

19. If we believe the Bible, and have faith in God, then why do we depend on our supervisors, spouses, and pastors instead of praying for expected outcomes?

20. We often think, "Satan is ignorant," is he really? What's the big deal if someone wants to take credit for something they have done?

21. Why is God so offended by what appears to be very innocent behavior on our part?

Chapter 6   WHO'S IN YOUR BOAT?

22. Who are storm starters and trouble makers? Have you ever allowed the wrong person in your inner-circle?

23. How can two people that are yoked together walk in different directions?

24. With friends like these who needs enemies, huh?

25. How low must God allow us to go, in effort to humble us, before we'll repent of pride?

COMING SOON
Additional Books by Author Cedric Oliver

- Manna Misconceptions -
An easy-to-read paperback that sheds light on a
God of great variety and abundance.
Manna Misconceptions will unveil an enlightening
mystery about giving thanks.
It'll also help readers take a leap of faith.

- Unlimited Kingdom -
This revelation will motivate readers to embrace
the reality that God has stretched human boundaries.
Now, Jesus Christ has empowered believers to
experience His promise of abundant life.

- Good Soil, Perfect Seed -
Oliver says God's word is perfect seed and the believers'
heart is good soil. This literary composition of biblical
metaphors will teach readers how to
produce a plentiful harvest.

Additional copies of this book and upcoming book titles
from REAP Publications are available at
www.embassiesofchrist.com

REAP Publications
900 West Ridge Road
Gary, Indiana 46408
219.887.6418